FLIGHT OF THE CONCHORDS

Contents

This book was approved by Flight of the Conchords

Album cover designed by Jeff Kleinsmith

Illustrations by Tyler Stout

Photos by Amelia Handscomb

Cherry Lane Music Company
Director of Publications/Project Editor: Mark Phillips
Project Coordinator: Rebecca Skidmore

ISBN 978-1-60378-101-5

Visit our website at www.cherrylaneprint.com

INTRODUCTION

Jemaine Clement   Bret McKenzie

How do you get someone to fall in love with you? Well, looking good helps, certainly. It's almost impossible to overstate the importance of the "physically attractive" factor within the love equation. But, what of the nugatory remainder? That miscellaneous two to two-and-a-third percent of the whole, which remains invisible to our Earth mirrors but accounts for one man's ease of contentment and dooms another to a life sentence of solitude.

I mean to say, what's up with that?

Take, as our case study, the world-famous New Zealand comedy and music duo Flight of the Conchords. Undeniably, they've got the goods in the face department. And yet, with our nation's recent emphases on proper diet, exercise, steroid abuse, and cosmetic surgery, that beauty stuff's as common as commas. No, the two antipodeans possess some unutterable and ultimately powerful else. An eldritch other, which has brought every woman of my acquaintance to discuss these two rogues in terms and tones more suited to the great classics of romantic literature. (Specifically, I'm thinking of certain titles I keep on an upper shelf, behind some luggage, in a plain cardboard box cleverly labeled "tax info.")

If near-universal wanton desire is any barometer of success, then truly, this is the era of Flight of the Conchords.

"Wherefore now? Why not sometime later? Next week, for example." It must be now, weary traveler, because as those selfsame troubadours have phrased it, "it's business time."

We begin with the two men in their younger years, Bret McKenzie and Jemaine Clement, students in Wellington, New Zealand, and the year of Flight of the Conchords' genesis, 1998 A.D. From there, things move quickly: regional shows, wider exposure, international comedy festivals, awards, respect, admiration, an eponymous HBO television series, and the captured hearts of a nation at large. (That was quick.)

Therefore, like any *Zeitgeist* worth its *Gewicht*, only one additional step rings logically sound: The Record Deal.

In the mid-summer of 2007, Sub Pop Records released a six-track Grammy Award–nominated (it's true!) CDEP, *The Distant Future*. Simply, it destroyed. Thus, it hath come to pass that a full-length album, helpfully titled *Flight of the Conchords*, has been recorded.

The record: produced by Mickey Petralia (Beck *Midnight Vultures*, Ladytron *Light & Magic*) in Los Angeles, New York, and Wellington. It features fully fleshed-out and professionally recorded versions of Flight of the Conchords concert and television favorites, rendering pointless all the inexpert fan-made audio transfers (the modern-day equivalent of holding a microphone up to the television speaker and shouting at your mom to be quiet), which have bloated hard drives the world over. The songs are heard here in expanded but reverent arrangements. Bret and Jemaine's trademark acoustic guitars lead the blitz, backed by a diverse array of instrumentation and production technique.

Agreed, the album sounds legitimate and musically, it's incredible, but, as Shakespeare said, "Does it funny?" Happily, yes. If amazing, delightful, and hilarious is your idea of funny, then prepare for undisappointment! These 15 songs pay homage to Pet Shop Boys, censorship, Marvin Gaye, sexism, Shabba Ranks, and backhanded compliments. To be blunt, if you can't find a *rire ou sourire* in the FSL study guide of opening track "Foux du Fafa," then, please notice, *vous êtes malade*.

You, if you do exist, have most likely already transferred the head with the heels for our two lads and need no further encouragement from my quarter to celebrate the release of this songbook. It must be nice to have someone to love, even if that love will never be returned. It must feel something like being alive. I'll never know. These cold, metal claws were programmed to perform only two functions: writing record company bios and killing humans. TTFN.

—M. W. Olsen

Foux du Fafa

Words and Music by
Bret McKenzie and Jemaine Clement

Amaj7   Dm/A   D7

Intro | Amaj7 | | | Dm/A | Amaj7 | |

Verse 1

Amaj7   Dm/A | Amaj7 |
    Je suis enchan - té.

Amaj7   Dm/A | Amaj7
Ou est le bibliothèque?

       | Amaj7   Dm/A |
Voilà mon pass - port.

Amaj7 | Dm/A |
    Ah, Gerard Depar - dieu.

Amaj7 | Amaj7   Dm/A | Amaj7
    Baguette,   ah ha ha hum. Baguette, ah ha ha oh oh oh oh.

Chorus 1

‖**Amaj7** |

Ba ba ba ba bow!   Foux du fa fa,

D7 |

       Foux du fa fa fa fa.

Amaj7 |

       Foux du fa fa,

D7 |

Ah ee ah.

Amaj7 |

       Foux du fa fa,

D7 |

       Foux du fa fa fa fa.

Amaj7 |

       Foux du fa fa,

D7

Ah ee ah.

Verse 2

                                 ‖**Amaj7**

Et maintenant le voyage à la supermarché!

   |**D7**

Pample - mousse.

     |**Amaj7**

Ananas.

     |**D7**

Jus d'orange.

    |**Amaj7**

Boeuf.

      |**D7**

Soup du jour.

     |**Amaj7**

Camembert.

      |**D7**

Jacques Cousteau.   Baguettte, oh!

Verse 3

```
     ‖ Amaj7                                                    |
Bon - jour. Bonjour. Bonjour. Bonjour, monsieur.
     D7
          Bonjour, mon petit bureau de change.
     | Amaj7
Ça va? Ça va. Ça va? Ça va.
          | D7                                                  |
Voi - là, le conversation à la parc.
     Amaj7
Ou est le livre? À la bibliothèque.
          | D7
Et le musique dance? À la discothèque.
          | Amaj7                                               |
Et les discothèques? C'est ici, bébé!
     D7                                                        ‖
Un, deux, un, deux, trois, quatre.
```

Chorus 2

```
     Amaj7                              |
          Foux du fa fa,
     D7                                         |
          Foux du fa fa fa fa.
     Amaj7                                   |
          Foux du fa fa,
     D7                                            |
Ah ee ah.
     Amaj7                                   |
          Foux du fa fa,
     D7                                              |
          Foux du fa fa fa fa.
     Amaj7                                   |
          Foux du fa fa,
     D7                                   ‖
Ah ee ah.
```

Verse 4

Amaj7 |
Ou est la piscine? Pardon moi?

D7 |
Ou est la piscine?   Uh.

Amaj7 |
     Splish, splash.   Uh.

D7 |
Eh. Ah. Je ne comprends pas.

Amaj7 |**D7** |
     Parlez-vous le français?   Eh?

Amaj7 |
     Parlez-vous le français?

D7 |**N.C.** | ||
   Uh,   non.   Hmmm.

Repeat Chorus 2

Outro   **Amaj7** |**D7** |**Amaj7** |**D7** |**Amaj7** ||

Inner City Pressure

Words and Music by
Bret McKenzie and Jemaine Clement

Gm   F   C   Cm   Am   Ab   D

134111   134211   32 1   13421   231   134211   132

Intro | Gm | F | C | | Gm | F | C | ||

Verse 1

Cm
Inner city life. Inner city pressure.

| **Cm**
The concrete world is starting to get ya.

| **F** |
The city is alive, the city is expanding.

F
Living in the city can be demanding.

| **Cm**
You pawned everything, everything you owned.

| **Cm**
Your toothbrush jar and a camera phone.

| **F**
You don't know where you're going, you cross the street.

| **F** |
You don't know why you did, you walk back across the street.

Cm
Standing in the sitting room, totally skint.

| **Cm**
And your favorite jersey is covered in lint.

| **F**
You want to sit down but you sold your chair.

| **F** | **Cm** |
So you,   you just stand there.

| **F** | ||
You just stand there.   You just stand   there.

Chorus 1

Gm |**F**
Inner,   inner city,

        |**C** |
Inner city pressure.

Verse 2

      ||**Cm**
Counting coins on the counter of the 7 - Eleven

    |**Cm**
From a quarter past six till a quarter to seven.

  |**F** |
The manager, Bevin, starts to abuse me.

F |
 Hey man, I just want some meusli.

Cm |
Neon signs, hidden messages.

Cm
Questions, answers, fetishes.

  |**F**
You know you're not in high finance.

   |**F** |
Con - sidering second-hand underpants.

Cm
Check your mind, how'd it get so bad?

    |**Cm** |
What happened to those other underpants you had?

F |
Look in your pockets, haven't found a cent yet.

F ||
Landlord's on your balls: "Have you payed your rent yet?"

Chorus 2

Gm   **|F**
Inner,   inner city,
     |C   **|**   **|**
Inner city pressure.
Gm   **|F**
Inner,   inner city,
     |C   **|**   **||**
Inner city pressure.

Interlude 1 **Am**   **|**   **|Ab**   **|**   **|**

           D   **|**   **|**   **|**
           Pressure.   Pressure.

Verse 3

     ||Cm
So you think maybe you'll be a prostitute.
     |Cm   **|**
Just to pay for your lessons, you're learning the flute.
F   **|**
Ladies wouldn't pay you very much for this.
F
Looks like you'll never be a concert flautist.
  |Cm
You don't measure up to the expectation.
     |Cm   **|**
When you're unemployed, there's no vacation.
F
No one cares, no one sympathizes.
  |F   **||**
You just stay home and play synthesizers.

Interlude 2   **Gm**   **|F**   **|C**   **|**   **|**

                       Gm   **|F**   **|C**   **|**   **||**
                       Pressure.   Pressure.

Repeat Chorus 2

Outro

       Gm   **|**
What are you searching for, hidden treasure?
F   **|C**   **|**
All you'll find is   inner city pressure.
         |Gm   **|**
You've lost perspective like a picture by Escher.

F   **|C**   **|**   **|**
  It's the pressure.
C   **|**   **|**   **|**   **|**   **||**

Hiphopopotamus vs. Rhymenoceros

Words and Music by
Bret McKenzie and Jemaine Clement

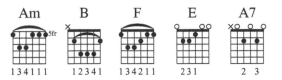

Intro   Am   B |F   E

Verse 1
                                  ‖Am   B
I'm the motherflippin'   rhymenocerous.
                                  |F
My beats are phat and the birds are on my back
         E
And I'm horny, I'm horny.
         |Am   B
If you choose to proceed, you will in - deed concede,
         |F   E
'Cause I hit you with my flow, the wild rhino stampede.

Verse 2
         ‖Am   B
I'm not just wild, I'm trained, domesticated.
         |F   E
I was raised by a rapper and rhino that dated
              |Am   B
And subse - quently procreated.   That's how it goes.
         |F   E
Here's the hiphopopotamus, the hip-hop hippo.

Chorus 1

         ‖**Am**   **B** |**F**   **E** |
They call me the   hiphopopotamus. My lyrics are bottomless.
Am   **B** |**F**   **E**   ‖

Verse 3

Am   **B**
Sometimes my rhymes are po - lite,
                       |**F**
Like "Thank you for dinner, Ms. Wright.
               E |
That was very de - licious. Good night."
Am   **B**
Sometimes they're obscene like a pornographic dream,
 |**F**   **E** |
NC-17 with ladies in a stream of margarine.
Am   **B** |
  Ha, ha, ha, ha, ha.   Yeah...
F   **E**
  Some margar - ine.

Chorus 2

        ‖**Am**
They call me the   hiphopopotamus,
B |
Flows that glow like phosphorous,
F   **E**
Poppin' off the top of this e - sophagus,
               |**Am**
Rockin' this me - tropolis.
             B
I'm not a large water-dwelling mammal.
                     E
      |**F**
Where did you get that preposterous hy - pothesis?
      |**Am**   **B** |**F**   **E**
Did Steve tell you that, perchance?   Hmm, Steve.

Verse 4

```
 ||Am                                  B
My rhymes and records, they don't  get played
        |F                                       E
Because my records and rhymes, they don't  get made.
        |Am                        B
And if you rap like me, you don't  get paid,
        |F                             E
And if you roll like me, you don't  get laid.
```

Verse 5

```
 ||Am                          B
My rhymes are so potent that in this small segment
          |F                    E                    |
I made all of the ladies in the area pregnant.
Am                    B
    Yes, sometimes my lyrics are sexist,
          |F                                E                              ||
But you lovely bitches and hos should know I'm trying to correct this.
```

Verse 6

```
Am            B            |
Other rappers diss me,
F                E          |
Say my rhymes are sissy.
Am            B            |
  Why? Why?    Why?
F                E
  Why exactly?   What? Why?
          |Am                      B                    |F          E          ||
Be more constructive with your feedback, please.   Why? Why?
```

Verse 6

```
          Am                    B
Why,  because  I  rap  a - bout  reality?
        |F                          E
Like  me  and  my  grandma  drinking  a  cup  of  tea?
        |Am              B              |
There  ain't  no  party  like  my  nana's  tea  party.
F        E          ||
  Hey!    Ho!
```

Outro

```
Am      B                        |
        I'm  the  motherflippin',
F      E                          |
        I'm  the  motherflippin',
Am      B                        |
        I'm  the  motherflippin',
F      E                              |
        Who's  the  motherflippin?
Am      B                        |
        I'm  the  motherflippin',
F      E                          |
        I'm  the  motherflippin',
Am      B                        |
        I'm  the  motherflippin',
F      E                  |A7              ||
        Motherflippin'.
```

Think About It

Words and Music by
Bret McKenzie and Jemaine Clement

Amaj7   F#m7   Bm7   D/E   Dmaj7   C#m7

Verse 1

|| **Amaj7**
There's children on the street using guns and knives;
F#m7
They're taking drugs and each others' lives.
Bm7
Killing each other with knives and forks
| **Bm7** | **D/E**
And calling each other names like "dork."   Oh, woh.

Verse 2

|| **Amaj7**
There's people on the street getting dis - eases from monkeys.
F#m7
Yeah, that's what I said, they're getting dis - eases from monkeys.
| **Bm7**
Now there's   junkies with monkey disease.
Bm7
Who's touching these monkeys, please?
Bm7
Leave these poor sick monkeys alone;
| **D/E**
They got problems enough as it is.

Verse 3

‖**Amaj7** |

A man is lying on the street; some punk's chopped off his head.

  |**F♯m7** | |**Bm7** |

I'm the   only one who stops to see if he's dead,

     |**Bm7** |**D/E**

Mm, turns out he's dead.

Chorus

                ‖**Dmaj7**

And that's why I'm singing: What,

     |**C♯m7** |

What is wrong with the world today?

Bm7 | |

  What's wrong with the world today?

Dmaj7 |**C♯m7** |**Bm7**

What, what is wrong with the world today?

     |**Bm7**   ‖

You gotta think about, think, think about it.

Verse 4

Amaj7 |

    Good cops been framed and put into a can,

      |**F♯m7** | |

And all the money that we're making is going to the man.

Bm7

    What man? Which the man? Who's the man?

     |**Bm7**

When's a man a man? What makes a man a man?

    |**Bm7** |**D/E**

Am I a man? Yes, technically I am.

Verse 5

||**Amaj7** |
They're turning kids into slaves just to make cheaper sneakers,
   |**F♯m7**
But what's the real cost?
     |**F♯m7** |**Bm7**
'Cause the sneakers don't seem that much cheap - er.
       |**Bm7**
Why are we still paying so much for sneakers
       |**Bm7** |**D/E**
When you got them made by little slave kids?   What are your overheads?

Verse 6

    ||**Amaj7** | |
At the end of your life you're lucky if you die.
F♯m7 | |
   Sometimes I wonder why we even try.
Bm7 |
   Saw a man lying on the street half dead
 |**Bm7** |**D/E**
With knives and forks sticking out of his leg.

Outro

    ||**Dmaj7** |**C♯m7** |
And he said,   ah ah ah wow wow wow wow wow wow.
Bm7 | |
   Can somebody get the knife and fork out of my leg, please?
Dmaj7 |**C♯m7** |**Bm7** |
   Can somebody please re - move these cutleries from my knees?
    |**Amaj7** | |
And then we break it down. *Ad lib to end*
N.C. | | | | | | | | | |

Amaj7 | |**F♯m7** | |**Bm7** | | |**D/E** |

Dmaj7 |**C♯m7** |**Bm7** |**Amaj7** ||

Ladies of the World

Words and Music by
Bret McKenzie and Jemaine Clement

Intro

Bbm7 | |Gbmaj7 |Cb7 ||

Chorus 1

Bbm7 |
Just wanna do something special
Bbm7 |Gbmaj7 |Cb7 |
For all the ladies in the world. Oh, yes.
Bbm7 |
Just wanna do something special
Bbm7 |Gbmaj7
For all the ladies in the world. Is that possible?
|Cb7
And the girls, don't forget them girls.

Verse 1

||Bbm7 |
Car - ibbean ladies. Par - isian ladies.
|Gbmaj7 |Cb7
Bo - livian ladies. Na - mibian ladies.
|Bbm7 |
Eastern Indo - chinian ladies. Republic of Do - minican ladies.
|Gbmaj7 |Cb7 ||
Am - phibian ladies. Presby - terian ladies.

Verse 2

B♭m7 |
Outta sight. Amazin' ladies.

B♭m7 |
Late night. Hard-workin' ladies.

G♭maj7
Erudite. Brainy ladies.

   |**C♭7** |
Herm - aphrodite. Lady-man ladies.

B♭m7 |
    Oh, you sexy hermaphrodite lady-man ladies,

               |**G♭maj7** |
With your sexy lady bits   and your sexy man bits too.

C♭7 ‖
Even you must be in to you, ooh ooh.

Bridge

Fm |
   All the ladies in the world,

E♭m |**C♭7**
   I wanna get next to you, show you some grat - itude

   |**C♭7** |
By makin' love to you; it's the least we can do.

Fm |
   If every soldier in the world

E♭m |**C♭7**
   Put down his weapon and picked up a wom - an,

   |**C♭7** |
What a peaceful world this world would be.

F5 |**E5**
    Redheads, not warheads.

     |**A♭** |
Blondes, not bombs.   Ooh, we're talkin' about

D♭m   **E♭** ‖
   Brunettes, not fighter jets.

Verse 3

B♭m7 |

          Oh, oh it's got to be

B♭m7 |

Sweet 16's, not M-16's

G♭maj7

When will the governments realize

 |C♭7 ||

It's got to be funky sexy ladies?

Verse 4

B♭m7 |

        I have a vision and all I can see

B♭m7

      Is all of you with all of me

  |G♭maj7

In a world of peace and harmony,

    |C♭7

Where every lady gets a little piece of Bret - y.

       |B♭m7

I've been to Paris, Wellington, and Amsterdam.

   |B♭m7

And wham-bam, merci, danke, thank you, ma'am.

     |G♭maj7

I don't care if you're ugly or you're skanky or you're small,

  |C♭7 ||

Just wanna do a little something special for y'all.

Chorus 2

B♭m7 |
    Just wanna do something special

B♭m7 |**G♭maj7**
    For all the ladies in the world.

                  |**C♭7** |
All the old ladies.   All the clean ladies.

B♭m7 |
    Just wanna do something special

B♭m7 |**G♭maj7**
    For all the ladies in the world.   All the crazy ladies.

   |**C♭7** |**B♭m7** |
And the girls,   don't forget them girls.   Ladies.

B♭m7 |**G♭maj7** |**C♭7** |
    Ladies.   Ladies.   Ladies.

B♭m7 | |**G♭maj7** |**C♭7** ||

Outro

Fm |**E♭sus2** |**C♭maj7** | |
Ah,   ah, ah,   ah, ah.

Fm |**E♭sus2** |**C♭maj7** | |
Ah,   ah, ah,   ah, ah.

Fm |**E♭sus2** |**C♭maj7** | |
Ah,   ah, ah,   ah, ah.

Fm |**E♭sus2** |**C♭maj7** | |**Fm** ||
Ah,   ah, ah,   ah, ah.

Mutha'uckas

Words and Music by
Bret McKenzie and Jemaine Clement

Am   C/G   F   E   Dm

Intro

Am	C/G	F	E	
Am	C/G	F	E	
Am	C/G	F	E		

Chorus 1

Am |C/G
Too many mutha'uckas 'uckin' with my   shi'.
    |F |E
There's   too many mutha'uckas 'uckin' with my   shi'.

('Uckin' with my shi'.)
Am |C/G
Too many mutha'uckas 'uckin' with my   shi'.   (With my shi'.)
F
How many mutha'uckas?
E
Too many to kill, mutha'uckas.

Verse 1

```
     Am                        C/G                  |
         I  pay  my  mutha'uckin'  rent  fortnightly.
     F                    E                    |
         Mutha'uckas  at  the  bank  trying  to  play  me,
     Am                        C/G                  |
         And  I'm  out  for  my  ac - count  'cause  out  on  A.P.
     F           E              |
     (On A.P.)  Yeah,    you  know  me.
     Am                      C/G                    |
         Mutha'ucka  charge  a  two-buck  transaction  fee.
     F                            E                        |
         Makes  my  payment  short,    my  rent  comes  back  to  me,
     Am                    C/G
         Minus  a  twenty-five       dollar  penalty.
      |F                       E                    |
     So  you'll  fee  me  'cause  of  your  mutha'uckin'  fee.
     Dm
         Read  the  words  on  my  ATM  slip;
                     |E                                              ||
     It  said  we're  all  mutha'uckas  and  we're  uckin'  with  your  shi'.  Come  on.
```

Chorus 2

```
     Am                                          |C/G
         Too  many  mutha'uckas  'uckin'  with  my     shi'.    (My  transaction  shi'.)
          |F                                        |E
     There's    too  many  mutha'uckas  'uckin'  with  my     shi'.
                                         |
     (My  weekly  statement  shi'.)
     Am                                          |C/G                          |
         Too  many  mutha'uckas  'uckin'  with  my     shi'.    (With  my  balance  shi'.)
     F                            |
         How  many  mutha'uckas?
     E                              ||
         Too  many  to  kill,  mutha'uckas.
```

Verse 2

```
        Am                        C/G
        The mutha'ucka runs a racist 'uckin' grocery.
        |F                       E
The mutha'ucka won't sell an apple to a Kiwi.
        |Am                C/G                    |
The shi'-fight's gonna get vicious and malicious.
F             E                      |
Cut the cra'. I need my red delicious.
Am                            C/G
        Tells me as a Kiwi that my money isn't valid.
            |F                       E                    |
Gonna dice the mutha'ucka like a mutha'uckin' fruit salad.
Am          C/G                      |
Then...         Granny Smith...
F             E     |Dm                    |
    An avocado...          a mango...
E                                          ||
    Then pop an apple in his ass, yeah!
```

Chorus 3

```
        Am                                   |C/G
        Too many mutha'uckas 'uckin' with my    shi'.

(I'm gonna juice the mutha'ucka.)
            |F                               |E
There's   too many mutha'uckas 'uckin' with my   shi'.
                                    |
(He's gonna wake up in a smoothie.)
Am                                   |C/G
    Too many mutha'uckas 'uckin' with my...
                      |F
Everybody, come on!
    |Am      C/G       F     E    |Am              ||
Yeah, too many mutha'uckas 'uckin' with my sh...
```

The Prince of Parties

Words and Music by
Bret McKenzie and Jemaine Clement

A	A7	A6	A5	C	G	Am	F

Intro A | A7 A6 A5 | A | A7 A | ‖

Verse 1

A |
I'm the pretty prince of parties,
A7   **A6**   **A5** |
You're a tasty piece of pastry.
A |
You're so lighty flighty flaky,
A7   **A** |
I go where the party takes me.

Interlude 1 A | A7 A6 A5 | A | A7 A | ‖

Verse 2

A |
I'm the funky monkey junky,
A7   **A6**   **A5** |
You're a flunky bunky donkey.
A |
You're a picture of the devil's daughter,
A7   **N.C.** | A | ‖
I'm a pitcher of holy water.

Bridge

```
          C                   G          |
      Oh, pretty prince   of parties,
  Am                   G                 |
  Where's the party now?   (I don't know.)
  C                   G          |
      Oh, pretty prince   of parties,
  Am                   G                 |
  Where does water go?   (I let it flow.)
  C                   G          |
      Oh, pretty prince   of parties,
  Am                   G          |
  Can I come to your party? (No.)
  C                   G          |
      Oh, pretty prince   of parties,
  Am                              G
  Where do you get your clothes?
                          |F        G        |A        |              ||
  They're made of snow. Pretty party clothes cro - chet of snow.
```

Interlude 2

```
  A                    |                  |                  |              ||
```

Verse 3

```
  A                          |
  I'm the Mickey, Maori Minstrel,
  A7                    A6    A5   |
  You're the high priest - ess of tinsel.
  A                          |
  I'm the guru god of ganja,
  A7    N.C                       |A              |A7    A6    A5   ||
  Rama - shalanka lanka ravi shanka.
```

Outro

```
  A                              |              |A7    A6    A5   |
  La la la la la la la la la la la la la la.
  A                              |              ||
  La la la la la la la la la la la la la la.
```

Leggy Blonde

Words and Music by
Bret McKenzie and Jemaine Clement

D   F♯   G   A   Gmaj7   G♯m7♭5   D5

Intro

D   F♯ |G   A

       |D   F♯ |G   A
Goodbye,
       |D   F♯ |G   A   ‖
Goodbye - ee - eye,   (leggy blonde).

Verse 1

D   F♯
Every day I look across the office floor, there you were,
   |G
Your hair down to your legs
       A |D   F♯
And your legs down to the floor.
       |G   A   ‖
Leggy blonde, goodbye,   goodbye.

Verse 2

D   F♯ |
Now that you are gone I'll never see you here for tech repair.
G   A
Wish you knew how much I loved your legs
     |D   F♯
And your hair.
     |G   A   ‖
Leggy blonde, goodbye,   goodbye.

Chorus 1

D   F♯ |
Leggy, leggy, leggy, leggy, leggy, leggy, leggy, leggy,
G   A |
Leggy, leggy, leggy, leggy, leggy, leggy, leggy, leggy.
D   F♯ |
Blondie, blondie, blondie, blondie, blondie, blondie, blondie, blondie,
G   A |
Blondie, blondie, blondie, blondie, blondie, blondie, leggy blonde,
D   F♯ |G   A   ‖
   Goodbye, goodbye.

Bridge

Gmaj7 |
  I had a budgie, but it died.
G♯m7♭5 |
  Woh, woh,
D |A | ‖
  I like pie!

Chorus 2

D   F♯ |
Leggy, leggy, leggy, leggy, leggy, leggy, leggy, leggy,
G   A |
Leggy, leggy, leggy, leggy, leggy, leggy, leggy, leggy.
D   F♯ |
Blondie, blondie, blondie, blondie, blondie, blondie, blondie, blondie,
G   A   ‖
Blondie, blondie, blondie, blondie, blondie, blondie, leggy blonde.

Interlude

D F♯ |G A |D F♯ |G A |

D F♯ |G A |D F♯ |G A ‖

Verse 3

```
       D                      F♯                          |
       I'll never get, I'll never get to be with you.
       G                         A                         |
       I'll never get to share an - other cup of tea with you.
       D                          F♯                        |
       I'll never get to let you know how much I think of you.
       G                         A                          |
       I'll never get to tear your clothes off on the photocopier.
       D                            F♯
       He'll never get, he'll never get, he'll never get,
                    |G         A           ||
       He'll never get to say...
```

Outro

```
       D5
       Hoop, leggy blonde, you got it goin' on
                                              |
       Wanna see you wearin' that thong thong thong.
       D5
       See you gettin' down till the break of dawn... panties on.
                    |D    F♯    |G    A    |D            ||
       Goodbye.
```

Robots

Words and Music by
Bret McKenzie and Jemaine Clement

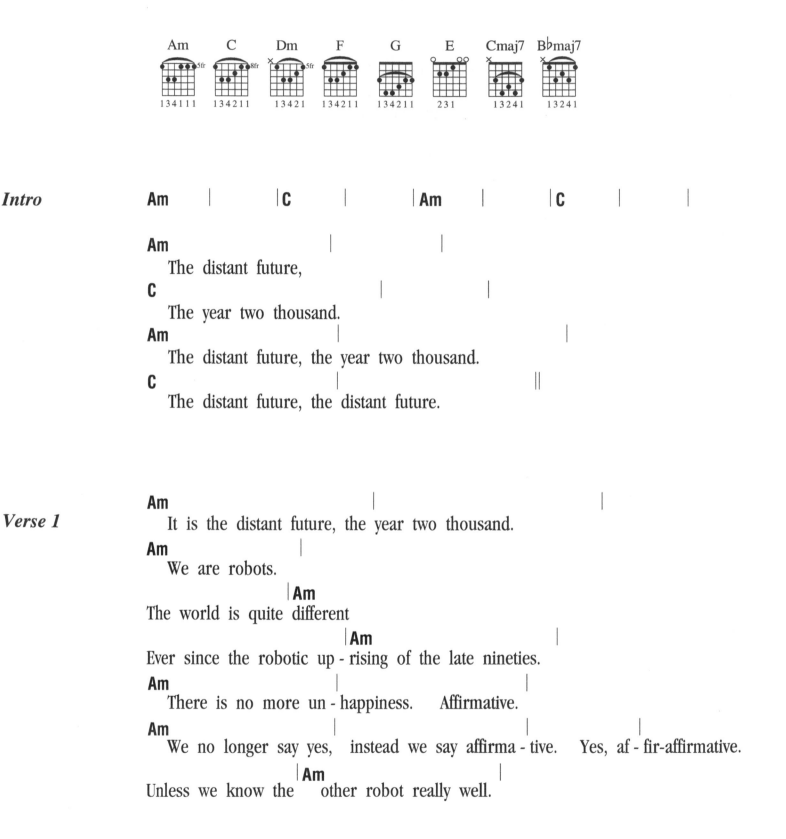

Intro

Am | | C | | Am | | C | | |

Am
The distant future,
C
The year two thousand.
Am
The distant future, the year two thousand.
C
The distant future, the distant future.

Verse 1

Am
It is the distant future, the year two thousand.
Am
We are robots.
Am
The world is quite different
Am
Ever since the robotic up - rising of the late nineties.
Am
There is no more un - happiness.   Affirmative.
Am
We no longer say yes,   instead we say affirma - tive.   Yes, af - fir-affirmative.
Am
Unless we know the   other robot really well.

|Am |
There is no more unethical treatment of the elephants.

Am | | |
    Well, there's no more elephants, so ...   Ah. But still it's good.

Am |
There's only one kind of dance,   the robot.

   |Am |
And the roboboogey. Oh, and the ro... two kinds of dances.

      |Am
But there are no more humans.

N.C. |
Finally robotic beings rule the world.

Chorus 1

      ‖Am |
The humans are dead.

     |Dm |
The humans are dead.

       |C |
We used poisonous gases.

      |Dm |
And we poisoned their asses.

   |Am |
The humans are dead.   (The humans are dead.)

   |Dm |
The humans are dead. (They look like they're dead.)

  |C |
It had to be done. (I just confirmed that they're dead.)

    |Dm   N.C.
So we could have fun. (Affirmative. I poked one; it was dead.)

Bridge 1

```
   ||F                          |G
Their system of oppression, what did it lead to?
   |Dm                       |C
Global robo depression, ro - bots ruled by people.
        |F                         |G
They had so much aggression that we just had to kill them,
     |F                    |E          |              ||
Had to shut their systems down.
```

Verse 2

```
   Am                  |
   Robo captain,    do you not realize
            |Am                              |                              |
That by de - stroying the human race because of their destructive tendencies,
Am                        |                        |
We too have become like...    well, it's ironic
Am                                 |
   Because we... (Silence, destroy him.)
```

Bridge 2

```
   ||F                              |G
After time we grew strong and developed cognitive powers.
        |Dm                     |C
They made us work for too long for un - reasonable hours.
    |F                                  |G
Our program being determined that the most efficient answer
     |F                            |E         |              ||
Was to shut their motherboard f**king systems down.
```

Bridge 3

    Dm |**G**
       Can't we just talk to the humans?
  |**Cmaj7** |**F** |
A little understanding could make things better.
Bbmaj7 | |**E** |
       Can't we talk to the humans and work together, now?
                      |
E   **N.C**
No, because they are dead.

Chorus 2

                 ||**Am** |
I said the humans are dead. (I'm glad they are dead.)
        |**Dm** |
The humans are dead. (I noticed they're dead.)
          |**C** |
We used poisonous gases (with traces of lead).
          |**Dm** |
And we poisoned their asses (actually their lungs).

Solo

               ||**Am** |
Binary solo: Zero, zero, zero, zero, zero, zero, one,
Dm |
Zero, zero, zero, zero, zero, zero, one, one,
C |
Zero, zero, zero, zero, zero, zero, one, one, one,
Dm |
Zero, zero, zero, zero, zero, zero, one, one, one, one,
Am |
Zero, zero, zero, zero, zero, zero, one,
Dm |
Zero, zero, zero, zero, zero, zero, one, one,
C |
Zero, zero, zero, zero, zero, zero, one, one, one.
Dm   **N.C.** ||
C'mon, sucker, lick my battery.

Outro

```
      Am         |Dm                          |
      Boogey,      boogey. (The humans are...)
      C          |Dm                              |
      Boogey,      roboboogey. (The humans are...)
      Am         |Dm                      |
      Boogey,      boogey. (Roboboogey.)
      C          |Dm                 |
      Boogey,      roboboogey.
      Am         |Dm                          |
      Boogey,      boogey. (The humans are...)
      C          |Dm                              |
      Boogey,      roboboogey. (The humans are...)
      Am         |Dm                  |
      Boogey,      boogey. (Roboboogey.)
      C          |Dm                          |Am
      Boogey,      roboboogey. (The humans are dead.)
      N.C.                    |
      Once again without e - motion,
                            |Am                                    ||
      The humans are dead, dead, dead, dead, dead, dead, dead, dead.
```

Boom

Words and Music by
Bret McKenzie and Jemaine Clement

Am   B♭m

134111   134111

Intro

Am
Oh, my god,

Am
She's so hot.

Am
She's so flippin' hot,

Am
She's like a curry.

Am
I wanna tell her how hot she is but she'll think I'm being sexist.

| **Am**
She's so hot, she's making me sexist.   Bitch.

| **Am**
I need my 1987 DG-20 Casio Electric Guitar

| **Am**
Set to mando - lin.   Yeah,   drop the drums.

Verse 1

‖**Am** |
I see you give the sign, I wanna boom like it's never been done.
Am |
   Bust a move at the click boom of a gun.
Am |
In the marquee and the bass is booming.
Am
Someone's smoking boom in da back of da room.
      |**Am** |
And it's the first day of boom, and the flowers are blooming.
Am |
Drum boom bass and the party is booming.
Am |
Boom ba boom like a rocket taking off to da moon.
Am   ‖
   Boom boom like a bride and groom, ah.

Verse 2

Am |
   See ya shaking that boom boom.
Am |
   See ya looking at my boom boom.
Am
   See you want some boom boom.
 |**Am** |
It's clear it's boom time boom boom.
Am |
   Let me buy you a boom boom.
Am |
   You order a fancy boom.
Am
You like boom, and I like boom,
 |**Am**   ‖
E - nough small boom, let's boom the boom, ah.

Verse 3

N.C. |

Fast forward selector.

B♭m |

Now we're rollin' on our boom boom, ah,

B♭m

Right into a my private room.

    |**B♭m**

And we know what's happenin'; we both assume

      |**B♭m**   ‖

We're gonna boom boom boom till the break of boom, ah.

Chorus 1

B♭m |

Who's the boom king? (Who?)

B♭m |

I'm da boom king. (What?)

B♭m |

Who's the boom king? (Tell me now.)

B♭m   ‖

I'm da boom king. (He's the boom King.)

Bridge

N.C. |

Chaka, Chaka, Chaka.   (Ha, ha, ha.)

N.C. |

Chaka, Chaka, Chaka. (Ha, ha, ha, ha.)

N.C. |

Chaka, Chaka, Chaka.   (Ha, ha, ha.)

N.C.

Chaka, Chaka, Chaka. (Ha, ha, ha, ha.)

Verse 4

‖**B♭m**
My phone is beeping; it's beep-booms-boom.
｜**B♭m**
He's back from ten years doom and gloom.
｜**B♭m**
And he said he had his boom chopped off in the boom,
｜**B♭m**
But the crazy boom still loves to boom.
｜**B♭m**
Un - zip the boom and my lens goes zoom.
｜**B♭m**
My beat boom drops ba da ba boom boom.
｜**B♭m**
We both get freaky and the boom gets squeaky
｜**B♭m**   ‖
And we boom boom boom boom boom boom boom.

Chorus 2

B♭m   ｜
Who's the boom king? (Who?)
B♭m   ｜
I'm da boom king. (What?)
B♭m   ｜
Who's the boom king? (Hah!)
B♭m   ｜   ‖
I'm da boom king. (Bret's the boom King.)

A Kiss Is Not a Contract

Words and Music by
Bret McKenzie and Jemaine Clement

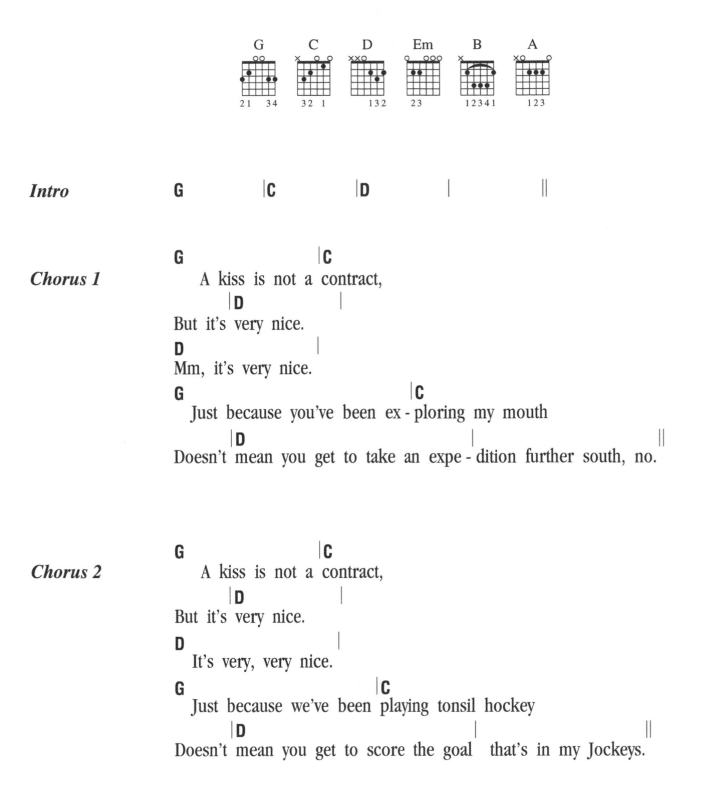

Intro

G |C |D | ||

Chorus 1

G |C
   A kiss is not a contract,
     |D |
But it's very nice.
D |
Mm, it's very nice.
G |C
   Just because you've been ex - ploring my mouth
     |D | ||
Doesn't mean you get to take an expe - dition further south, no.

Chorus 2

G |C
   A kiss is not a contract,
     |D |
But it's very nice.
D |
   It's very, very nice.
G |C
   Just because we've been playing tonsil hockey
     |D | ||
Doesn't mean you get to score the goal   that's in my Jockeys.

Verse 1

Em | |D
        Just be - cause I'm in a two-man novelty band
      |D |C
Doesn't mean it's all about poontang.
|C |B
I can't go around loving everyone;
 |B |A ||
I just wouldn't get anything done.

Verse 2

Em | |D
        You can take me out to dinner; that might be quite nice.
      |D |C
You could buy me a burrito and some beans and rice.
   |C |B |
But that won't get you into pants paradise.
  |A |
They call it a fly because it takes you up to heaven.
 |G |C |D | ||
Oh, oh.

Chorus 3

G |C
  A kiss is not a contract,
   |D |
But it's very nice.
D |
  It's very, very nice.
G |C |
  I'm only one man,
D | |
  Baby,   pretty baby.
G |C |
  We're only two men, ladies,
D | |G |C D |G ||
  Babies,   pretty babies.

40

The Most Beautiful Girl (In the Room)

Words and Music by
Bret McKenzie and Jemaine Clement

Dmaj7 Amaj7 Bm/E A6 A7 Dm/A Bm D

Intro

| Dmaj7 | Amaj7 | Bm/E | A6 | A7 |

| Dmaj7 | Amaj7 | Bm/E | A6 | A7 |

| Dmaj7 | Amaj7 | Bm/E | A6 | A7 |

Verse 1

Dmaj7   Amaj7 |Bm/E
  Look 'round room; I can tell that you
   A6 A7 |Dmaj7 Amaj7 |Bm/E
Are the most beautiful girl in the   room,
   A6 A7 |
In the whole wide room. Ooh.
Dmaj7   Amaj7 |Bm/E
  And when you're on the street, depending on the street,
   A6 N.C. | |
I bet you are definitely in the top three
Dmaj7   Amaj7 |Bm/E
Good-looking girls on the street. Yeah,
   A6 A7 ||
Depending on the street.

Verse 2

```
       Dmaj7                                 Amaj7
             And when I saw you at my mate's place
              | A6                   | N.C.
       I thought, What  is  she  doing
              | Dmaj7
       At my mate's place?
       Amaj7              | Bm/E              A6        A7         | Dmaj7
       How did Dave get a hottie like that to a party like this? Good one, Dave!
       Amaj7                     | Bm/E          A6    A7      |
             Ooh, you're a leg  -  end, Dave!
       Dmaj7                         Amaj7                           |
             I asked Dave if he's going to make a move on you.
       Bm/E                          A6        A7        | Dmaj7
             He's not sure. I said, "Dave, do you mind if I        do?"
            Amaj7                |
       He says he doesn't mind,
             | Bm/E                        A6          A7       |
       But I can tell he kinda minds, but I'm gonna do it anyway.
       Dmaj7                         Amaj7               |
             I see you standing all a - lone by the stereo.
       Bm/E                         A6      N.C.          ||
             I dim the lights down to very low; here we go.
```

Chorus 1

```
       Dmaj7          Amaj7                      |
             You're so beautiful  (beautiful),
       Bm/E                      A6      A7      |
       You could be a waitress.
       Dmaj7          Amaj7                 |
             You're so beautiful  (beautiful),
       Bm/E                      A6      A7      | Dmaj7
             You could be an air host - ess in the six   -   ties.
            Amaj7                  |
       You're so beautiful,
       Bm/E                  A6    A7  | Dmaj7     Amaj7
             You could be a part - time  model.
            | Bm/E                 A6              A7          ||
       And then I seal the deal: I do my moves, I do my dance moves.
```

Interlude   **Amaj7**   **|Dm/A**   **|Amaj7**   **|Dm/A**   **‖**

Bridge

Amaj7   **|**
It's twelve - oh - two, just me and you,
Dm/A   **|Amaj7**
And seven other dudes around you on the dance floor.
                                |
I draw you near. "Let's get outta here.
Dm/A   **‖Dmaj7**
Let's get in a cab, I'll buy you a ke - bab!"

Verse 3

                        Amaj7   **|Bm/E**   **A6**   **A7**
Now, I can't be - lieve that I'm sharing a kebab with the most beautiful girl
    |Dmaj7   **Amaj7 |Bm/E**   **A6**   **A7**   **|**
I have ever seen with a kebab.   Ooh.
Dmaj7   **Amaj7**
"Why don't we leave?
  |Bm/E   **A6**   **A7**   **|**
Let's go to my house and we can feel each other up on the couch."
Dmaj7   **Amaj7**   **|Bm/E**
Oh, no. I don't mind taking it slow - ho - ho,
    A6   **A7**   **‖**
No - ho - ho, yeah.

Chorus 2

Dmaj7   **Amaj7**
'Cause you're so beautiful,
  |Bm/E   **A6**   **A7**
Like a tree,
      |Dmaj7   **Amaj7**   **|**
Or a high - class prostitute. You're so beautiful,
Bm/E   **A6**   **A7** **‖Bm**
Mm, you could be a part - time model.

Outro

|D
But you'd probably still have to keep your normal job.

|Bm
A part-time model!

|D   N.C.
Spending part of your time modeling and part of your time

|Dmaj7 Amaj7 |Bm/E   A6   A7 |Dmaj7 Amaj7
Next to me,

|Bm/E   A6   A7 |Dmaj7 Amaj7 |Bm/E
And the rest of your time doing your normal job.

        A6   A7 |Dmaj7 Amaj7 |Bm/E A6 A7 |
My place is usually tidier than this.

Dmaj7   Amaj7 |Bm/E   Amaj7   ‖

Business Time

Words and Music by
Bret McKenzie and Jemaine Clement

Gm   Cm   Dm   G   Gm6

134111   13421   13421   134211   13 141

Intro   **Gm** | | | **Cm** **Dm** ‖

Girl,

Verse 1

Gm

Tonight we're gonna make love.

|**Gm** |

You know how I know?   Because it's Wednes - day,

|**Gm**   **Cm**   **Dm**

And Wednesday night is the night that we usually make love.

|**Gm**

Monday night is my night to cook,

|**Gm**

Tuesday night we go and visit your mother,

|**Gm** | **Cm** **Dm** ‖

But Wednesday   we make sweet, weekly love.

Verse 2

Gm

That's when everything is just right.

Gm

There's nothing good on TV,

Gm

You haven't had your after-work social sports team practice,

So you are not too tired.

Gm

Oh, boy,   it's all on.

Gm

You lean in and whisper something sexy in my ear like,

|Gm

"I might go to bed now. I've got work in the morning."

Gm

I know what you're trying to say, girl.

| Gm   Cm Dm |Gm

You're trying to say "Oh, yeah,   it's business time,

| Gm   G ||

It's business time."

Cm

Chorus 1   It's business,

Dm |Gm

It's business time.   I know what you're trying to say.

|Gm

You're trying to say it's time for business. It's business time, ooh.

Cm

It's business,

Dm |Gm |Gm6 ||

It's business time.

Verse 3

Gm

Then we're in the bathroom   brushing our teeth.

 |Gm | **Cm Dm** |**Gm**

That's all part of the foreplay, I love foreplay.

Gm

Then you sort out the recycling.

 |Gm

That isn't part of the foreplay process, but it is still very important.

Gm

Next thing you know, we're in the bedroom.

  |Gm

You're wearin' that baggy old ugly T-shirt

 |Gm

You got from your work several years ago.

Gm

Mm, you know the one, baby,   with the color stain.

Verse 4

Gm

I remove my clothes very, very clumsily,

Gm

Tripping sensuously over my pants.

Gm

Now I'm naked except for my socks,

                     |Gm |N.C.

And you know when I'm down to just my socks   what time it is.

Chorus 2

Cm

It's business,

Dm |Gm

It's business time.   You know when I'm down to my socks

     |Gm

It's time for business. That's why they're called business socks, ooh.

Cm

It's business,

Dm |Gm |Gm6

It's business time.

Bridge

```
Gm                      |
    Making love,
Gm                          |
    Making love for,
Gm                              |
    Making love for two,
Gm                                  ||
    Making love for two minutes.
```

Verse 5

```
Gm                                      |
    When it's with me, girl, you only need two minutes
                    |Gm              |
Because I'm so    intense.
    |Gm                                  |
You whisper something sexy like, "Is that it?"
Gm                                  |
    I know what you're trying to say, girl.
Gm                                      |
    You're trying to say, "Oh, yeah, that's it."
Gm
    And you tell me you want some more.
    |Gm              |              |          ||
Well, uh, I'm not surprised,      but I'm quite sleepy.
```

Chorus 3

```
Cm              |
    It's business,
Dm                  |Gm
    It's business time.
                        |Gm          |
Business hours are over,   baby.
Cm              |
    It's business,
Dm                  |Gm      |Gm6      |Cm          |Dm      |
    It's business time.
Gm          |          |Cm      |Dm      |Gm      ||
```

48

Bowie

Words and Music by
Bret McKenzie and Jemaine Clement

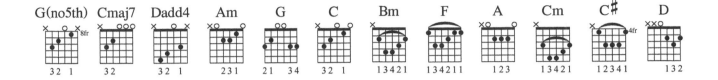

Intro

      G(no5th)   **Cmaj7** |**Dadd4**   **Am**
      Bowie's in space.

      G(no5th)   **Cmaj7** |**Dadd4**   **Am**
      Bowie's in space.

     |**G(no5th)**   **Cmaj7**
Whatcha doin' out there, man?

   |**Dadd4**   **Am**
That's pretty freaky, Bowie. (Ooh, Bowie.)

  |**G(no5th)**   **Cmaj7**
Is it cold out in space, Bowie?

                  |**Dadd4**
You could borrow my jumper if you like, Bowie.

        Am |**G(no5th)**
Does the cold of deep space make your nipples get pointy, Bowie?

    Cmaj7
Do you use your pointy nipples

  |**Dadd4** |**G(no5th)**
As telescopic antennae transmitting data back to Earth?

       Cmaj7 |**Dadd4**
I bet you do, you freaky old bastard, you.

Am |**G(no5th)**   **Cmaj7**
Do you have one really funky sequin spacesuit, Bowie?

    |**Dadd4**
Or do you have several ch - changes?

     Am
Do you smoke grass out in space, Bowie?

G(no5th)   **Cmaj7**
    Or do they smoke astroturf? Ooh.

Interlude

N.C. |
      Recieving transmission from David Bowie's nipple antennae.
      |
Do you read me, Lieutenent Bowie?
           | |
I said, do you read me, Lieutenent Bowie?
G | | | ‖

Verse 1

G |
   This is Bowie to Bowie.
       |**C** | |
Do you hear me out there, man?
Dadd4   **|C**
    This is Bowie back to Bowie.
|**G** | |
I read you loud and clear, man.   Ooh, yeah, man!
  |**G** |**C**
Your signal's weak on the radar screen.
              |**Dadd4**
How far out are you, man?
     |**C** |**G** |
I'm pretty far out. That's pretty far out, man!

Pre-Bridge

       ‖**Am**
Ooh - ah - ooh.
       |**Am**
I'm orbiting Pluto.
      |**Bm**
Ooh - ah - ooh.
       |**Bm** |**C**
Drawn in by its groovitational, groovitational pull.
           |**C**
I'm jamming out with the Mick Jagger-nauts.
      |**G**   **F**   **A**   **F** | ‖
And they think it's pretty cool, man.

50

Bridge

```
        F                                       |Am
            Are you okay, Bowie? What was that sound?
                                           |Cm
        I don't know, man; I have to turn my ship around.
                                 |G
        Ooh, it's the craziest scene.

                                       |C♯
        Yeah, I'm picking it up on my LSD screen.

                           |A                      |
        Can you see the stratosphere  ringing
        D                   |                    ||
        To   the   choir   of  Afro-nauts singing?
```

Outro

```
        G            |            |
            Bowie's in   space.
        C                |                    |
        Bowie,    Bowie,    Bowie, Bowie, Bowie, Bowie.
        G            |            |
            Bowie's in   space.
        C                |                    |
        Bowie,    Bowie,    Bowie, Bowie, Bowie, Bowie.
        G                      |                |
        Eenie, I'm a meenie mynie mowie.
        C                        |
        Eenie, I'm a meenie mynie mowie.
                           |G          ||
        B-b-b-b-b-Bowie's in        space.
```

Au Revoir

Words and Music by
Bret McKenzie and Jemaine Clement

Dm7   G7   Cmaj7   Fmaj7   B♭maj7   Bm7   E7

Verse 1

Dm7 |**G7** |
     Au revoir,

Cmaj7 |**Fmaj7** |
     Au revoir,

B♭maj7 | |
     Au revoir,

Bm7   **E7**   ‖
     Au re - voir.